Kane/Miller Book Publishers, Inc.
First American Edition 2009
by Kane/Miller Book Publishers, Inc.
La Jolla, California

First published in France under the title: *Mes images du Japon*
© Editions du Sorbier, 2007

All rights reserved. For information contact:
Kane/Miller Book Publishers, Inc.
P.O. Box 8515
La Jolla, CA 92038
www.kanemiller.com

Library of Congress Control Number: 2008933428
Printed and bound in China
1 2 3 4 5 6 7 8 9 10
ISBN: 978-1-933605-99-9

My Japan

Etsuko Watanabe

Kane/Miller
BOOK PUBLISHERS

My name is Yumi and I'm seven years old. My family and I live in a house
in the suburbs of Tokyo. I'm in my room. Can you see me?

My Bedroom

This is my room. I share it with my little brother Takeshi. (He's five.)
We have bunk beds – I sleep on the top bunk.
I'm packing my school bag for tomorrow.

School Bag: Girls have red ones, and boys have black ones. We keep the same bag all through school.

Desk: I keep my school things in the right drawer. The one in the middle is my secret drawer.

Lamp: We turn it on and off by pulling the string.

In Japan, we sleep on futons. They are light and very easy to fold and carry.
When you air them out in the sun, they feel warm and fluffy.
Mmmm, very nice to sleep on!

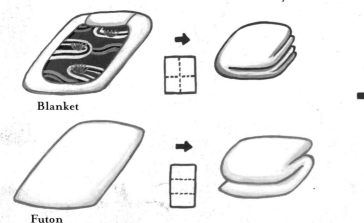

Blanket

Futon

Painted Closet: We store our futons in here during the day.

In the Kitchen

I love to cook with my mother.
We chop, we mix, we season, we grill ... and best of all, we eat!

だいどころ

Omuraisu

Sushi

Hamburger

Yakizakana

Okosama Ranchi

Tonkatsu

Kare Raisu

Ramen

Zaru Soba

Udon

Tempura

Spaghetti

Sukiyaki

Yakitori

Korokke

Fried Rice

Gyoza

Our Bathroom

ふろば

Do you hear that? My father is singing in the bathtub. Our whole family loves to sing. Look at Takeshi — he's washing all by himself, just like a grown-up.

1 First, fill the tub with warm water — it will stay warm, thanks to the lid.

2 Make sure to wash off with a soapy washcloth and clean water.

3 Now it's time to relax and soak in the tub. The whole family will use the same water.

Ladle, for pouring water and rinsing off.

Washcloth, for washing off the dirt.

Stool

Mat, so we don't slip … or get cold feet!

Western Toilet:
The buttons control the seat temperature and also the water and hot air (for washing and drying bottoms).

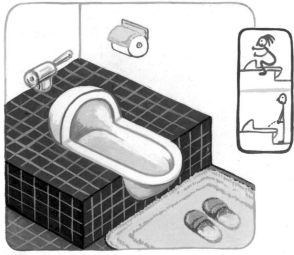

Japanese Toilet:
These are harder to use. Don't forget to wear the slippers! They help keep everything germ-free.

The First Day of School

しんがっき

School starts in April, when the cherry trees bloom.
Takeshi has a new uniform — he's starting kindergarten.
I'm going to primary school. It's a little scary,
but I'm going to learn lots of new things.

Takeshi's School Things (For Kindergarten)

School ID Badge

Slippers

Summer Uniform

School Shirt

Castanets

Gym Clothes

Plastic Cup

Lunchbox

Modeling Clay

Pastels

Yumi's School Things (For Primary School)

Red Leather School Bag

School ID Badge, with Yumi's address and blood type in case of an accident.

Slippers

Gym Clothes

School Envelope, to hold Yumi's lunch and activities money.

Cloth

School Books

Harmonica

Pencil Case

Paint Box

The School Day

We walk to school in the morning with our neighbors. Taro is the oldest, so he watches out for us.

When we get to school, we take off our shoes, put them in our cubbies, and change into slippers.

We greet our teacher at the start of class.

I love music.
We learn lots of songs.

がっこうせいかつ

We have gym outside in the courtyard.
There's also a pool, so we have
swimming lessons too.

We take turns serving lunch.
(Today is my turn.) I sit at the same table
as Mrs. Tanaka, my teacher.

Everyone helps to clean the school.
Every day we clean the classrooms, the
bathrooms, the halls and the courtyard.

I walk home from school with
my friend Yuka. See you tomorrow!

Summer Vacation

なつやすみ

Hooray! It's summer vacation, the first big holiday of the school year.
We're going to Nagano, where my grandparents live. Summer is very hot
and sometimes very wet, but there are a lot of things to do.
I love watching the fireworks. There are celebrations in the temples, too.

Fireworks

Incense, to keep the
mosquitoes away.

Paper Fan

Electric Fan

Yukata, a traditional summer
kimono made of cotton.

Geta, wooden
sandals.

Wheat Tea

Bell, to ring in
the breeze.

Stag Beetle: Children love these bugs
and keep them as pets. You can buy
them in most big department stores.

Jinbe: It looks like a yukata,
but it has two pieces
and no belt.

Daruma Doll: You paint one eye
when you make a wish and the other
eye when the wish comes true.

The Public Bath

I love going to the public bath. It's the perfect place for whispering secrets with my friend Yuka. What's funny is that in every public bath I've been to, Mount Fuji is painted on the wall.

Here's what to do:

- Take off your shoes and put them in a locker.
- Make sure you go in the right door
  (men = otoko, women = onna).
- Buy your ticket at the front desk.
- Take off your clothes and leave them in the locker room. Don't forget your locker key!
- Pick a stool and a basin, and wash yourself carefully before getting into the bath.

Wonderful! You are doing things just right!

Transportation

こうつう

You can travel around Tokyo by bus, taxi or the subway — but be careful! In Japan there are no street names, only district names. If you have to go somewhere, you'd better know the way.

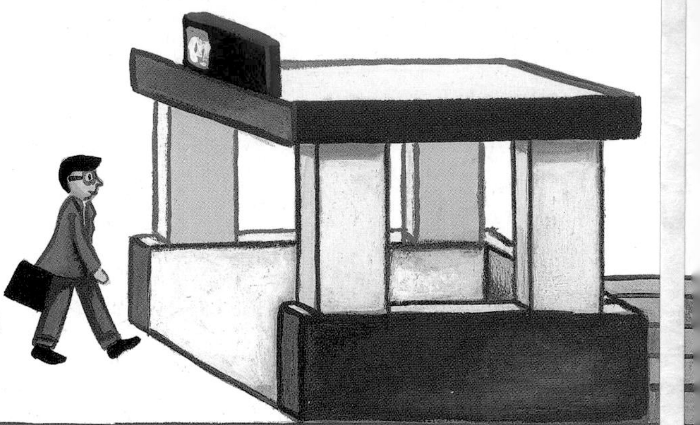

WC

It's Sunday, and the department stores are open so everyone can go shopping. Sometimes the busiest streets are closed to traffic, making them perfect for strolling!

おおみそか

December 31st

On the last day of the year we declare
war on dust and clean the whole house.
Everything has to be perfect for the New Year.

Our dad cleans his office.

Takeshi and I clean the windows.
Sometimes we use old newspaper.

On New Year's Eve, tradition says
we must eat buckwheat noodles.
They are long and thin — a symbol
of longevity.

At midnight all the bells in all
the temples in Japan toll one
hundred and eight strokes.
Happy New Year!

January 1st

The first day of the year is a very special day.
We make decorations and play games, and there is delicious food.
My mother always makes mochi. Lots of people make and eat
these rice cakes for the New Year. I love them!

しょうがつ

Osechi-ryori: Colorful dishes packed in layered lacquer boxes. Each dish and ingredient in Osechi has meaning.

Kagami Mochi: A dish made of two mochi, offered to the gods the first day of the year.

Ozoni: A traditional mochi soup served on New Year's Day.

Karuta: A Japanese card game, often using poems.

New Year's Gifts: Children receive these special envelopes filled with money.

Greeting Cards: These must arrive on New Year's Day — the postal service waits until then to deliver them.

Top

Kadomatsu: A lucky charm usually placed by the home's entrance.

Kite

Hanetsuki: A Japanese game, similar to badminton.

Fukuwarai: A game like Pin the Tail on the Donkey — except in Fukuwarai, players pin on parts of a face.

ひなまつり

March 3rd, Girls' Day

March 3rd is Hinamatsuri, Girls' Day. This tradition comes from the Heian period, when dolls given to the princess were thought to prevent illness and curses. A few weeks before this special day, I place my dolls on a red platform. They represent the old court's emperor and empress and their attendants.

Make a doll's dress.

The day after Girls' Day, we put all our dolls away. They say if you leave them on the platform you'll never get married!

May 5th, Children's Day

May 5th is Kodomo No Hi, Children's Day or Boys' Day. Takeshi places samurai weapons on a stand and hangs a carp flag. The carp symbolizes strength and perseverance, qualities we wish for the boys.

Make a samurai hat.

July 7th, Tanabata

July 7th is Tanabata. Legend tells us that one day a weaving princess fell in love with a young cattleman. Enraged, the gods forbade the princess and the cattleman to meet again. The pain the two endured was so great that the gods took pity on them. Once a year, during Tanabata, they allow the cattleman and the princess to cross the Milky Way and meet each other.

Orihime, the weaving princess

Make a paper streamer.

Hikoboshi, the cattleman

Every July 7th we write a wish on a colored piece of paper and hang it from a bamboo branch. On this day when the cattleman and the princess are allowed to meet again, they are so happy they make every wish come true. I can't tell you my wish — it's a secret!

Write down your wish.

Make a paper chain.

Make a paper lantern.

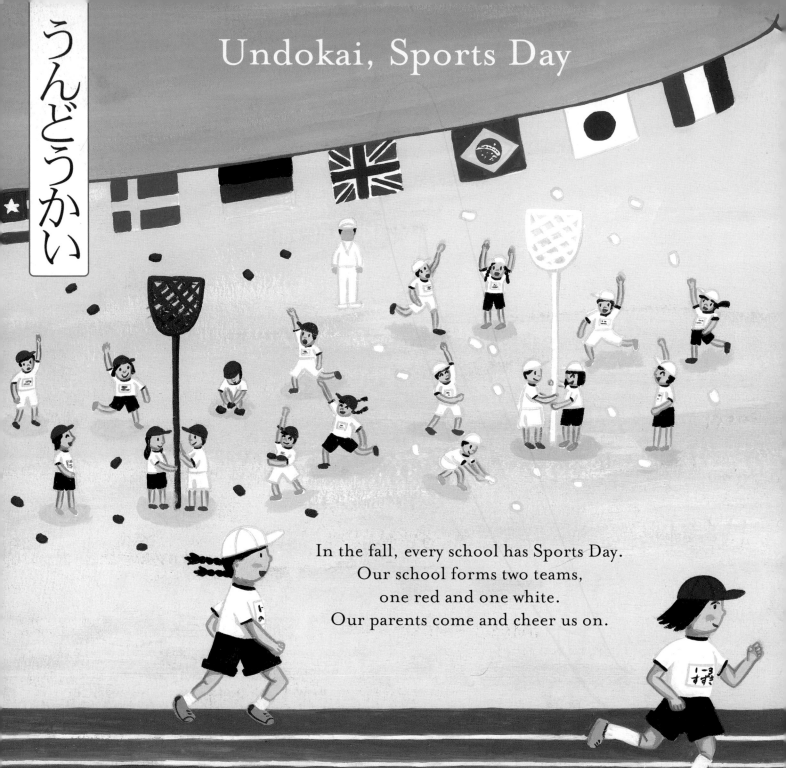

Undokai, Sports Day

うんどうかい

In the fall, every school has Sports Day.
Our school forms two teams,
one red and one white.
Our parents come and cheer us on.

The different events might include running, tug-of-war, human pyramids or three-legged races. Each teaches us how to work as a team and shows us how much stronger we are when we all work together.

Shichi-Go-San

しちごさん

In November we celebrate Shichi-Go-San, Seven-Five-Three Day. We wish good health, happiness and longevity to three and seven-year-old girls, and three and five-year-old boys. This year, since I am seven and Takeshi is five, the two of us will wear our best kimonos and visit the temple with our parents.

Under my kimono I wear nagajuban.

My fancy hairclips

My socks

My fan

My shoes

My little fabric bag

I put on my kimono and accessories.

Takeshi wears his kimono. He has his fan, his knife and his traditional shoes.

I tie my kimono with an obi, a large belt of colored fabric.

Writing

There are three different kinds of writing in Japan:
kanji, hiragana and katakana. Kanji are ideograms representing words.
In primary school we have to learn at least one thousand of them.
Here are some kanji, and how they came to be:

Yama
Mountain

Kawa
River

Ki
Tree

Hi
Sun

Tsuki
Moon

Hiragana represent syllables. So do katakana, but we use katakana to write foreign words. Here is the hiragana table. It has to be read from top to bottom. Try writing my name, Yumi. You'll see, it's not easy!

ん	わ	ら	や	ま	は	な	た	さ	か	あ
n	wa	ra	ya	ma	ha	na	ta	sa	ka	a
(い)	り	(い)	み	ひ	に	ち	し	き	い
(i)	ri	(i)	mi	hi	ni	chi	shi	ki	i
(う)	る	ゆ	む	ふ	ぬ	つ	す	く	う
(u)	ru	yu	mu	hu	nu	tsu	su	ku	u
(え)	れ	(え)	め	へ	ね	て	せ	け	え
(é)	re	é	me	he	ne	te	se	ke	(é)
を	ろ	よ	も	ほ	の	と	そ	こ	お
wo	ro	yo	mo	ho	no	to	so	ko	o